IT'S ALWAYS ABOUT THE CHILDREN

Charles A. Barrett

It's Always About the Children

Published by

CAB Publishing Company, LLC

PO Box 422

McLean, Virginia, 22101

© 2018 Charles A. Barrett

ISBN-13: 978-0-692-17457-9

ISBN-10: 0-692-17457-5

ACKNOWLEDGMENTS

The following individuals provided constructive feedback to help make this book what it is today. They are excellent professionals in their respective fields and I am grateful for their friendship and willingness to share in this process.

Lisa Cylar Barrett, JD
Managing Director, Federal Policy
PolicyLink

Eshé Collins, JD
Member
Atlanta Board of Education

Katherine Cowan
Director, Communications
National Association of School Psychologists

Worokya Duncan, EdD
Director of Inclusion and Community Engagement
The Cathedral School of St. John the Divine

Denise Ferenz
Director, Publications
National Association of School Psychologists

Benjamin Fernandez, MS, Ed
Coordinator, Prevention Services
Loudoun County Public Schools

Barbara Fromal, MEd
Eligibility Coordinator
Loudoun County Public Schools

Erin Harper, PhD
Assistant Professor
Texas A&M Commerce

Angela Manning, MEd
Teacher
Loudoun County Public Schools

Virginia Minshew, EdD
Retired Principal
Loudoun County Public Schools

Tammy Haegele, MEd
Educational Diagnostician
Loudoun County Public Schools

Angelica Parent, MEd
Educational Diagnostician
Loudoun County Public Schools

Rosalyn Pitts, PhD
School Psychologist
Atlanta Public Schools

Alan Skubal, MS
Teacher
Loudoun County Public Schools

Sherrie Proctor, PhD
Associate Professor of School Psychology
Queens College, City University of New York

Valerie Schwinger, MA, CCC
Retired Speech/Language Pathologist
Freeport Public Schools

Brittney Williams, MEd
Graduate Student
Temple University

Kelly Vaillancourt Strobach, PhD, NCSP
Director, Policy and Advocacy
National Association of School Psychologists

DEDICATION

Rev. Bruce Ferguson (d. 2004)
To an extraordinary champion and advocate for young people whose humility and life impacted me in immeasurable ways. Your consistent support, encouragement, and numerous opportunities to use my gifts have been instrumental in my development and will always be cherished.

To the amazing children, families, schools, and communities that I've had the pleasure of serving as a practicum student, intern, and school psychologist. You have taught me so much about courage, commitment, and resilience in the face of seemingly insurmountable obstacles. I have been enriched as a person and am a better psychologist because of you.

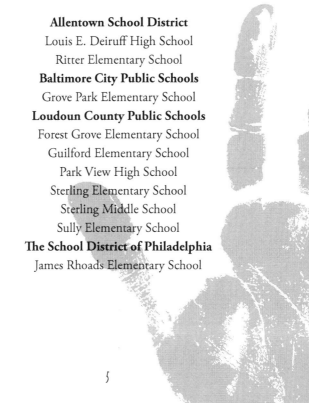

Allentown School District
Louis E. Deiruff High School
Ritter Elementary School
Baltimore City Public Schools
Grove Park Elementary School
Loudoun County Public Schools
Forest Grove Elementary School
Guilford Elementary School
Park View High School
Sterling Elementary School
Sterling Middle School
Sully Elementary School
The School District of Philadelphia
James Rhoads Elementary School

CONTENTS

ABOUT THIS BOOK

As I reflect on 10 years as a school psychologist, it is never quite comfortable for me to say that this is my job. Although it is the best career in the world, both by my standards and according to *US News & World Report*[1], school psychology is more than a profession. For me, and many of you reading this book, school psychology is a calling. And if you're not a school psychologist, because you serve children as a teacher, administrator, school social worker, school counselor, speech pathologist, or educational diagnostician, your vocation is a calling as well. Like a perfect union—a marriage between compatible individuals—school psychology found me, and I found school psychology. We were made for each other and I was destined to become a school psychologist. As much as I enjoy teaching undergraduate and graduate students and presenting to a variety of audiences at state and national conferences, the core of my professional identity is that of a school psychologist. I am a practitioner who serves real children and real families attending real schools in real communities. It is the joy and honor of being intimately involved in the lives of young people that informs all of my professional endeavors, including writing this book.

In early 2018, it occurred to me that a hashtag I started using—#itsalwaysaboutthechildren—was more popular than I realized. After a few friends and colleagues mentioned it, coupled with numerous professional experiences of my own, I was compelled to write about my passion for serving children. Although this book includes some technical information about the clinical aspects of school psychology and education in general, its focus is not what we do as educators. As one of the greatest benefits of effective instruction is teaching students how to think rather than what to think, this book is a window into my philosophical orientation to the fields of school psychology and public education. Amidst what feels like the inevitability of increasing demands that compete for our time and attention with each passing year, anecdotes are shared to highlight how fulfilling it is for me to serve children of all ages. I am confident that each chapter will inspire, remind, and rejuvenate us about our most important responsibility: children.

Although this book is most relevant to practitioners, faculty, and graduate students in school psychology, it is also fitting for teachers, school counselors, school social workers, educational diagnosticians, and speech pathologists. Building and central office administrators (e.g., principals, special education and pupil services directors) as well as graduate faculty in related disciplines may also find the content useful for their staff and students. To facilitate dialogue about the ideas presented, questions for reflection and small group discussion are included at the end of each chapter. Additionally, *References and Resources for Professional Learning* allow interested readers to further explore the concepts mentioned throughout the book.

From one colleague to another, whether you are entering the field of education, have been serving for a few years, or nearing the end of your career, thank you for your commitment to children. Thank you for the countless ways that you ensure their academic, social, emotional, and behavioral well-being.

And most of all, thank you for making eternal deposits into the lives of young people who will shape our future and make us proud by the great things that they are destined to accomplish.

Because it's always about the children,

CAB

Please think of the children first. If you ever have anything to do with their entertainment, their food, their toys, their custody, their childcare, their health care, their education—listen to the children, learn about them, learn from them.

Think of the children first[2].

—Fred Rogers

CHAPTER 1

THIS IS MY STORY:
PURPOSE, PASSION, HOPE, AND WHOLENESS

And while we don't always know exactly where our purpose
comes from, it is often clarified through our experiences.
What we have encountered and overcome allows us to help
others be better.

Everyone has a story. You have a story and I have a story as well. In serving children, we should never underestimate the significance of our stories. What may not be learned through the most eloquent lessons or masterfully implemented group or individual counseling sessions, children grasp through the human connection that is forged in sharing lived experiences. Some may refer to this as building rapport; but it is simply the power of relationship that leads to the most effective instruction and positive outcomes.

While teaching one evening, I shared with my community college students that it took me longer than I anticipated to complete my PhD. A simple moment of transparency led to their faces lighting up with surprise, interest, but most of all, hope. As many of my students are English Learners (ELs) who are also juggling the responsibilities of working full-time and raising children, they are managing more than I ever had to contend with in undergraduate or graduate school. From this short exchange, I learned a profound lesson: students genuinely want to know who their teachers are as people. In the words of James Comer, noted child psychiatrist and advocate for education reform, "No significant learning occurs without a significant relationship[3]." Regardless of our roles as educators, our first responsibility is to establish relationships with our students. A little transparency does not change the fact that we are the professionals. It simply builds a bridge to our students because they see us as humans. With that in mind, this is my story.

GROWING UP

My earliest recollection of wanting to work with children was in high school. Especially for a person whose friends were almost always adults, this was somewhat surprising to me. While I don't know where this interest came from, it was quite evident by my junior year. Having always enjoyed English and writing, after flirting briefly with a career in print journalism—I specifically remember thinking that I wanted to become the editor of the *New York Times*—I decided to become a high school English teacher.

As a youngster, and to some degree today, I stuttered. Between first and sixth grades, I participated in school-based speech therapy. Throughout elementary school, my speech teacher was Ms. Valerie Schwinger. She was patient, kind, and taught me a lot—some of which I continue to use today. If my aspirations of becoming an English teacher did not work as planned, I would become a speech pathologist to help children like me. Although I was very comfortable with my decision, an opportunity presented itself that I could not ignore.

A few months before graduating high school, I heard about the Initiative for Minority Student Development (IMSD) program at St. John's University. Federally funded by the National Institutes of Health (NIH), it sought to prepare undergraduates for research careers in the biomedical sciences; increase the number of underrepresented minority undergraduates who chose to major in biomedically-related sciences; and raise the awareness among underrepresented minorities majoring in the sciences to consider biomedical research as a desirable career. Knowing that I was not particularly excited about a career in biomedical research, I was not interested in the program. However, as my father and I were meeting with the program coordinator and Timothy Carter, the faculty member who was responsible for the grant, they mentioned that psychology and sociology were also acceptable majors for participation in the program. Despite planning to study English and speech pathology, because IMSD provided full tuition, a stipend, and up to six credits of summer classes each year, I ultimately changed speech pathology to psychology in order to take advantage of this opportunity.

THE COLLEGE YEARS

Having indicated my interest in psychology, Dr. Carter gave me a catalogue that contained the research of the St. John's faculty. After looking through it, I identified a few professors who were studying topics that I was at least open to learning more about. Dr. Carter called one of them, who was the chair of the psychology department. Although he was not accepting students to work with him, he told us about Raymond DiGiuseppe whose research on anger and aggression in adolescents was intriguing to me. My father and I met with Dr. DiGiuseppe and he agreed to work with me.

Following my first year in college, I was a camp counselor in the Catskill Mountains. Although my tuition was covered, and I was receiving a stipend, like most college students, I needed to make a little extra money over the summer. After spending seven weeks with intelligent, creative, and energetic boys, if there was any lingering doubt in my mind, I absolutely knew that I had to work with children.

Near the end of my undergraduate career, I did not know what I wanted to do. After all, three years is not a lot of time to figure out the rest of your life! While I knew that I wanted to work with children, I was still unsure of how I would use my degrees in English and psychology. Did I still want to become an English teacher? Did I eventually want to become a principal or even a superintendent? What about a child psychologist? I spoke to Dr. DiGiuseppe about my uncertainty and everything changed in one brief conversation. He asked me if I had ever considered school psychology. I had not. In fact, I had never heard of school psychology. He said that it was a relatively new field, but he thought that I would like it based on my interests in children, psychology, and education. After Dr. DiGiuseppe told me that he was a clinical child and school psychologist, I was convinced that school psychology was for me! Not knowing where to apply to graduate school, he told me about Lehigh University. And because I trusted him, I set my sights on Lehigh.

GRADUATE SCHOOL

To say that my first semester in graduate school was a huge learning curve would be an understatement. Having never taken any education courses, and only being somewhat familiar with school psychology, many of the terms and concepts were foreign to me. What was an IEP? What was an FBA? What was IDEA? In addition to finding myself in a puzzling world of alphabet soup, my biggest question was *is this what I really want to study?* Perhaps it was because I was only 20 years old and had very little life or professional experiences that I began to doubt whether I made the right decision to pursue school psychology. And despite my many questions, I had very few answers.

For those of you who have earned, or are pursuing a doctoral degree, especially a PhD, a significant amount of time in graduate school is dedicated to research. Because of this, having at least a general idea of your research interests sooner than later is very helpful. Serendipitously, my senior thesis as an undergraduate was on Attention Deficit Hyperactivity Disorder (ADHD). Specifically, I reviewed a paper by Reid, DuPaul, Power, Anastopoulos, Rogers-Adkinson, Noll, and Riccio[4] about the cultural factors that are involved in assessing children and adolescents for this condition. Not knowing a lot about ADHD, and much less about school psychology, I remember asking George DuPaul at my interview for the school psychology program at Lehigh if he was the same DuPaul whose work I had been reading. He was. What began as intellectual curiosity about why Black males seemed to be diagnosed with

ADHD and placed in special education more than other groups became central to my development as a psychologist.

PURPOSE, PASSION, HOPE, AND WHOLENESS

In life, and specifically as an undergraduate, graduate student, and professional, none of our experiences are ever wasted. Everything happens for a reason. Through childhood events, family situations with parents and siblings, volunteer and professional opportunities, overcoming learning challenges and other disabling conditions, or marriage and raising children, our lives evolve and afford us greater clarity about what we should be doing. My passion for serving children grew out of having a speech impediment and working with Black boys at a summer camp. But while passion is necessary for personal and professional fulfillment, it is not sufficient. Passion must be informed by purpose.

My purpose in life is not to be a school psychologist. Although this sounds antithetical to who I am, what I enjoy doing, and the book that you are reading, purpose is greater than position. Purpose is the reason for our existence, which cannot be contained by what we are currently doing. In other words, school psychology, teaching, and counseling are simply ways that we fulfill our purpose; but in and of themselves they are not why we exist. My purpose is to communicate and facilitate hope and wholeness. Whether through writing, teaching, or serving children, families, schools, and communities as a school psychologist, I am driven by helping people have hope of better days ahead and becoming whole despite experiencing brokenness. And while we don't always know exactly where our purpose comes from, it is often clarified through our experiences. What we have encountered and overcome allows us to help others be better.

As a child who stuttered, I have learned that my speech impediment was not a speed bump—something to slow me down—but a stepping stone. It made me more sensitive to others, not only those with speech impediments, but people who are different for various reasons. In my undergraduate and graduate courses, I require my students to speak in every class session. But because I stutter, I intentionally and quickly create a supportive environment that is conducive for students to feel comfortable sharing their ideas, asking questions, and responding to their peers and me. Because I stutter and know what it feels like to prefer listening rather than contributing verbally, I am sensitive to my EL students who may be self-conscious about their English proficiency. I am sensitive to shy students whose anxiety makes it difficult to present to their peers. Stuttering has made me more patient because I wanted others to be patient with me. It has made me a better listener because I needed others to listen to me more intently when I was a youngster. It has made me a better psychologist—one who is slow to form impressions because all students deserve this from the adults in their lives. Having met with parents and students who stutter, I understand that they are quiet, not because they do not know the answer or do not want to contribute, but because they may be nervous.

Even decisions that I felt were made for pragmatic reasons were ultimately purposeful and led me to where I am today. Changing my major from speech pathology to psychology was more than benefiting from an opportunity that would fund my undergraduate education. Participating in the IMSD program was the catalyst that introduced me to Raymond DiGiuseppe—a man who mentored me into the field of school psychology and is why I am a school psychologist today. Working at a summer camp, seemingly to make a little extra money, was a pivotal experience that crystallized my desire to serve children. In fact, it was the first time that I realized children always give us more than what we think we are giving them. While I thought that I was simply going to make a few hundred dollars over the summer, my life was forever changed and my purpose and passion for children was confirmed. Studying ADHD in Black males throughout graduate school provided an invaluable foundation for my current scholarship and professional passion: a deep interest in the assessment practices that are used to identify culturally and linguistically diverse (CLD) students with a variety of disabilities.

CHAPTER SUMMARY

More than an autobiographical retelling of life experiences, this chapter highlights the interconnectedness of where we have been and where we are today. Because seeing is believing, when young people see what we have accomplished, they believe that they can do these things as well. Regardless of our respective roles as educators, our stories expose children to the possibilities of what they can achieve and become.

As we think about our lives and decisions to work with children, consider these two questions: what led me to a career in education? Further, why do I want to serve children? As educators, why is almost always greater than what. More than what we do, the underlying purpose for our actions is of utmost importance. Especially when balancing the inevitable challenges that are associated with working in public education, understanding why we are teachers, administrators, school counselors, school social workers, educational diagnosticians, speech pathologists, and school psychologists helps us to remain focused and true to our commitment: excellent service to children, families, schools, and communities.

REFLECTION AND DISCUSSION

1. Watch the following video: https://www.youtube.com/watch?v=1ytFB-8TrkTo[5]. How is this concept applicable to education, and more specifically, your respective discipline?

2. Based on the video above, think about why you are a teacher, administrator, school psychologist, school social worker, school counselor, educational diagnostician, or speech pathologist. Record your thoughts in the space provided below. If you are comfortable, share these with your classmates or colleagues.

3. For graduate educators: Consider having your students write and present about why they chose their respective discipline (e.g., school psychology, school counseling, social work, teaching, administration), their emerging beliefs about the field, the populations they are interested in serving, and their professional goals. Additionally, have them write about their philosophical orientation to serving students, families, schools, and communities as a professional. Having assigned these activities to graduate students in school and developmental psychology, they are helpful exercises that challenge trainees to think about why they chose the field, how their past experiences shape their beliefs about the field, and how they approach serving students, families, schools, and communities.

REFERENCES AND RESOURCES FOR PROFESSIONAL LEARNING

1. Best Jobs Rankings. *U.S News & World Report.* Retrieved from https://money.usnews.com/careers/best-jobs/school-psychologist

2. Dockray, H. (2018, June). 15 Mister Rogers quotes for when you need a friendly neighbor. *Mashable.* Retrieved from https://mashable.com/2018/06/13/mister-rogers-best-quotes/#vgqHEzUNbqq3

3. Comer, J. P. (2001). Schools that develop children. *The American Prospect, 12,* 30-35.

4. Reid, R., DuPaul, G. J., Power, T. J., Anastopoulos, A. D., Rogers-Adkinson, D., Noll, M., & Riccio, C. (1998). Assessing culturally different students for Attention Deficit Hyperactivity Disorder using behavior rating scales. *Journal of Abnormal Child Psychology, 26,* 187-198.

5. Jr., Michael. (2017 January 8) *Knowing Your Why?* [Video file]. Retrieved from https://www.youtube.com/watch?v=1ytFB8TrkTo

CHAPTER 2

SERVING FAMILIES AND SCHOOLS:
THE OVERLOOKED CLINICAL SKILLS

People don't care how much you know until they know
how much you care[1].

In serving students, families, schools, and communities, we are susceptible to thinking that we have all of the answers to the myriad issues facing children. Perhaps it is because we are passionate about what we do and invest ourselves in our work. And while we are often well-intentioned and have spent significant time and resources developing our skills to be more than competent educators, if we are not careful, our skills go unnoticed and ultimately the children whom we seek to help suffer.

Some of the information that will be presented in this chapter is covered, at least to some degree, in school psychology consultation courses. However, for my colleagues in related disciplines, you may not have been exposed to methods of collaborating with families, teachers, and other professionals to support the academic, social, emotional, and behavioral needs of children. For a review of evidenced-based behavioral consultation models[2], interested readers are encouraged to consider the *References and Resources for Professional Learn-*

ing at the end of this chapter. Following a brief explanation of the nature of schools, information will be presented in three sections: customer service, effective collaborative behaviors, and benefits for everyone.

THE NATURE OF SCHOOLS

Schools are some of the most politically-charged environments. In this context, political is not meant to be associated with partisan politics or political affiliation (e.g., Democrat, Republican, Independent), but institutions that are significantly influenced by power dynamics, structures, and hierarchies. While other industries' politics are often influenced by money, the nature of politics in schools is not necessarily economics, but the emotional investment that is inevitability associated with children. For school psychologists, effectively working with families, teachers, and administrators involves managing relationships with multiple individuals, some of whom may have competing interests. Especially for those of us who enjoy a great deal of flexibility and autonomy while serving several schools, we must intentionally cultivate and maintain relationships in order to position ourselves to share our knowledge and expertise in support of children.

CUSTOMER SERVICE

Every industry has a client. For educators, who is the client? Who is the beneficiary of our services? Consistent with the consultation literature, while the consultee is situationally dependent, the child is always the client. In other words, school psychologists collaborate with families in some instances, but also work closely with teachers and administrators in other circumstances.

Nevertheless, in all cases, as consultants working to develop the skill sets of our consultees, positive outcomes for children is the ultimate goal.

EFFECTIVE COLLABORATIVE BEHAVIORS

SPEND TIME DEVELOPING AN UNDERSTANDING OF THE SCHOOL CULTURE

The manner in which we begin our consultative relationships with consultees is critically important. Before offering intervention ideas to families, teachers, and staff, school psychologists should spend time thinking and learning about the following:

1. What do the students, families, teachers, and administrators in my school value? Are there differences in what these respective groups view as important?

2. What is my school's philosophical approach to instruction, discipline, and partnering with families? Are punitive approaches (i.e., suspension and expulsion) preferred rather than restorative practices?

3. How do teachers and administrators view effective instruction, differentiation, and intervention in reading, writing, and math?

4. How does my school support students who are not meeting grade level expectations?

5. How are data used to inform subsequent decisions about instruction and social, emotional, or behavioral support?

6. What are teachers' and administrators' understanding of Multi-Tiered Systems of Support (MTSS) and Response to Intervention (RtI)?

7. How are students with disabilities supported and provided access to the general education curriculum? To what extent are inclusion models preferred over exclusionary practices?

While not an exhaustive list, these questions show that there is no one-size-fits-all approach to serving students, families, schools, and communities. School psychologists who are cognizant of this reality position themselves to understand the unique perspectives of their diverse constituent groups and utilize their training to support the identified needs. Especially for early career and very experienced psychologists, one of the most detrimental missteps is superimposing our recent training in best practices, or what has worked in previous settings, on our current placement. Thoughtfully developing an understanding of the culture is time well spent.

LISTENING IS GREATER THAN SPEAKING

In the words of my grandmother, *we have two ears and one mouth. Therefore, we should listen twice as much as we speak.* Although a lighthearted comment, its truth resonates with me, especially as a school psychologist. Relatedly, perhaps you have seen a picture on the Internet of two individuals looking at the same image. From one person's perspective the picture is clearly the number 6. But to the other person, it is equally clear that it is the number 9. For obvious reasons, not only are both individuals correct, but this example underscores that different is not necessarily synonymous with wrong.

When collaborating with families and teachers, effective school psychological practice involves first listening to and validating their concerns. Sensitive school psychologists recognize that more than answers to their questions, clinical interpretations for their children's or students' presenting challenges, intervention suggestions to remediate a variety of skill and performance deficits, implications for next steps, or feeling that they are correct, individuals want to be heard and know that their concerns are reasonable. While seemingly unnecessary, validating families' and teachers' perspectives makes it exponentially easier to not only disagree with them, but to also offer ideas that they are more likely to consider. When school psychologists prematurely make suggestions before acknowledging and validating a family's or teacher's concerns, despite having a reasonable interpretation for the youngster's difficulties, it ultimately does not matter. Defensiveness and resistance take the place of openness to new ideas. A simple statement such as, "Sir, ma'am, I understand what you're saying. And what you're saying makes sense to me. However, another reason for the difficulty that [insert the child's or student's name] is experiencing at home or school is…" goes a long way.

Even after observing students, school psychologists and others who do not regularly spend time with children in their classrooms or at home should be mindful of dismissing families' and teachers' concerns because they did not personally witness the target behaviors. Remembering the principles of observer effects and demand characteristics, which assert that our presence in students' natural environments renders them no longer natural, are helpful to frame comments in ways that are both respectful and helpful to those with whom we seek to collaborate.

A LESSON FROM KENNY ROGERS

Some of the most popular lyrics from Kenny Rogers' *The Gambler*[3] are also fitting for school psychologists. *You've got to know when to hold 'em, know when to fold 'em. Know when to walk away...* At times we have very strong professional feelings about decisions that are being contemplated by multi-disciplinary teams. For example, if you have not already, you will likely work with a family or teacher who is advocating for a special education evaluation despite the available data suggesting otherwise. In these situations, we should ask ourselves the following questions:

1. Could my analysis of the data or situation be incomplete, or perhaps wrong?

2. And because I could be wrong, is it worth being inflexible, especially when the other team members are equally passionate about their position? Note: This is even more relevant if additional data could be collected that would be helpful to the discussion and subsequent decision. For example, it is almost always advisable to refer a student for an evaluation and allow the additional data to inform the most appropriate next steps.

Having been in these situations over the years, evaluating the student can lead to one of two possibilities. First, our impressions could be confirmed and the student does not have an educational disability. If this happens, we have not won. Instead, we are better positioned to help teachers understand the factors involved in determining special education eligiblity and how they can effectively meet the needs of their students. Remember: most teachers do not have the specialized training and experience in identifying disablities and would greatly appreciate learning more about the process. Further, the nature of people is that they sincerely want to understand how and why decisions are made. Rather than assuming that teachers are being difficult and disregarding what we are saying, school psychologists should listen to their concerns for their students, patiently explain our perspective, and move forward in the best interest of the child.

On the other hand, it is possible that our preliminary analysis was incorrect and the student does have an educational disability. Regardless of our knowledge and experience contributing to these decisions, we ultimatley do not know whether students are eligible to receive special education services until we have completed a comprehensive evaluation. For this reason, remaining somewhat tentative about our impressions not only shows humility and grace, but it communicates that we value families and teachers for their intimate understanding of their children and students. On one occassion, I was evaluating a student for whom anxiety seemed to be the primary referral concern. However, after reviewing his file, I spoke with his mother and she shared valuable information that challenged my thinking and prompted additional assessments. After evaluating a few more cognitive abilities, the mother's impressions were correct. The child actually had a Specific Learning Disability (SLD) and his anxiety was secondary to his underlying academic difficulty.

Although time-consuming, in order to develop the most accurate understanding of students' difficulties, it is important to speak to parents about their concerns for their children. Despite having our own ideas about what is contributing to students' difficulties, we must remain open to other perspectives, knowing that nothing will ever take the place of listening to families. While we do not have to know all of the answers, we must accept that parents at times know more than we do.

THE IMPORTANCE OF ASSUMPTIONS

While completing my graduate training, one of my practicum placements was in a diverse suburban school system. Working with a very experienced school psychologist, I learned one of the most valuable lessons of my budding career. My supervisor told me that he assumed all parents want the best for their children. This sentiment continues to resonate with me and influences how I practice today. Believing that parents—although they may not attend every parent-teacher conference, school event, or meeting—are unequivocally invested in their children's success, helps us to guard against our preconceived notions based on their observable behavior. When serving families who are forced to contend with the burden of limited financial resources, sensitive school psychologists frame their absence from school happenings as having nothing to do with their lack of interest in their children's education, but rather a function of the competing demand to provide food, clothing, and shelter. This rationale is also applicable to how school psychologists partner with teachers and administrators. Assuming that our colleagues are dedicated individuals who also have a vested interest in young people's success, the manner in which we interpret their behavior becomes quite different. Could it be that seemingly aggressive teachers—who want children evaluated due to the suspicion of an educational disability—may not be trying to circumvent the need for intervention and differentiated instruction, but genuinely believe that they are acting in the best interest of their students?

School psychologists have been trained to consider multiple sources of data to formulate the most accurate conclusions. Such consideration involves an awareness of our own, albeit subtle, assumptions that ultimately impact how we interact with consultees. Instead of criticizing and discounting families and teachers for behaviors or perspectives that may not be completely aligned with what we have come to acknowledge as best practices, we should help them to more effectively meet the needs of their children and students. As several individuals discussing a child are often communicating the same message, effective school psychologists identify common ground between all stakeholders while keeping what is best for the child priority.

THE NATURE OF THE FIELD IS SERVICE

School psychologists have the honor of being involved in work that can change the course of history. Moreover, the opportunity to collaborate with adults who will be instrumental in shaping students' social, emotional, behavioral, and academic development is humbling. The children whom we serve today will be faced with the challenges of civic leadership within our communities, the fiscal responsibility of our local and national economies, the weight of fostering a climate of respectful and inclusive politics, and the social well-being of our global society. For these and many other reasons, the work of school psychologists transcends a job. The untold benefit of our contribution for generations to come speaks to school psychologists as more than scientists and practitioners. Although profoundly understated, school psychologists are best understood as servants.

In serving students, families, schools, and communities, there are not many phrases that are more appropriate than "People don't care how much you know until they know how much you care[1]." Whether good or bad, after we have been hired, our colleagues assume that we possess the requisite competencies and credentials to adequately fulfill our job responsibilities. However, we will never be able to use our skills in child and adolescent development; social, emotional, and behavioral functioning; academic and cognitive assessment; and preventative mechanisms for a host of difficulties if we do not know how to work with people. For this reason, it is imperative that school psychologists become a part of their school communities.

While serving an elementary school, volunteering for morning and afternoon bus duty remains one of the most valuable and beneficial experiences of my career. A new psychologist, I did not know what to do on the first day of school. Working with an assistant principal who was also new to his position, we learned many aspects of our jobs together. Standing outside as buses arrived allowed me to learn a lot about the students, their families, and the community. It afforded me informal face time as I got to know parents on their terms. Rather than families coming inside to meet me, I went outside to meet them. Bus duty also showed them who I was as a person, which was more important than my position as the school psychologist. Serving a school with a significant Latino population, I quickly learned that the term psychologist was culturally loaded. Whereas White families were generally not intimidated by my title, some Latino families were uncomfortable as they associated my child is crazy with the term psychologist. Over time, I realized that allowing all families to see me as the man who shook their hands and greeted their children before and after school was tremendously helpful in diffusing their anxieties and making them more comfortable discussing their children's difficulties with me. In fact, over the course of 10 years, there are parents with whom I still keep in touch that I met while on bus duty. For staff, this showed them that I was a team player—a person who did not see himself as above certain duties but was willing to work with them on a rather mundane and non-preferred task. Because I was seen as involved in the school community, invested in its students and families, and supportive of teachers and staff, all of which were unrelated to the technical skills necessary for being a school psychologist, they were more open to implementing interventions. Rather than being told to do something by someone who did not know who they were, how much they cared about their students, and how hard they were working to ensure their success, I believe that teachers saw me as a colleague who could be helpful.

As stated earlier, there is no one-size-fits-all approach to serving schools. Because each building is different and has its own culture, we must be careful to figure out how we can become involved in the school and community without getting in the way. Although I was serving four schools at the time, my regular bus duty activities were only at one school. Not only was it impractical to be in four places at once, but my other schools did not necessarily have a need for me in this capacity. However, at another elementary school, my involvement and investment were shown through participating in its *Early Bird Reading* program. As students arrived before school to read, I met them in the cafeteria and placed a charm on their backpacks. This was helpful as I learned the names of students, some of whom were discussed in various meetings due to academic, social, emotional, or behavioral challenges. Rather than simply being a name to me, I knew them. These types of activities also inform our clinical practice. By getting to know teachers in both instructional and extra-curricular settings, we understand them as individuals and their approaches to students and instruction. We learn about intervention programs that are available at schools, which assists us in making more appropriate recommendations.

Being mindful of how we are perceived as school psychologists, managing these perceptions, and intentionally becoming enmeshed in the school culture is helpful for everyone. Like teachers, families will also ask for our input: *[insert your name] what do you think about this situation with [insert child's name] at home? What can I do to help them to be more successful?* Parents and teachers are more interested in our ideas when they see that we genuinely care about their children and students.

EVERYONE BENEFITS

You are likely familiar with Oprah Winfrey, the billionaire media mogul, talk show host, actress, producer, philanthropist, and her iconic September 2004 *Oprah Winfrey Show* episode in which she gave her entire 276-member audience brand new cars[4]. However, her exuberant and repeated exclamations of, "You get a car!" overshadowed the significance of this moment in television history. More than receiving new cars, the audience members' excitement was because a need was met in their lives. In other words, each individual was creatively and intentionally selected by the show's producers based on needing a car. Tears of joy and shouts of happiness had less to do with receiving something new, than it was about filling a void.

And so it is with serving students, families, schools, and communities: we must meet their needs. Defensibly the most famous triangle in psychology, Abraham Maslow's Hierarchy of Needs[5] shows that when individuals' basic needs are not met, it is more difficult for them to experience the other necessary needs. If children are hungry and tired, or don't feel safe in their homes and neighborhoods, how can we expect them to be available for reading, writing, and math instruction? As noted teacher and education activist Nicholas Ferroni has said, "Students who are loved at home come to school to learn; and students who aren't come to school to be loved[6]." Meeting children where they are—whether through establishing a trusting relationship or working with community resources to ensure that they have food to eat and a safe place to sleep—and helping them to meaningfully participate in their education is the joy of the profession. Regardless of our position, as we identify areas of need and work to address them, we will be more effective in our service to students, families, schools, and communities.

CHAPTER SUMMARY

Through spending time in schools, I have learned that some educators—principals, teachers, school psychologists—have not been taught how to work with people. While some industries place practice before people, the nature of education is relationships and people are always the priority.

This chapter did not provide any technical competencies for being an effective school psychologist, teacher, administrator, school social worker, or school counselor. If you are a graduate student, you are in the process of developing these skills. As a professional, you will continue to grow with experience and mentoring. Instead, this chapter explored professional behaviors and a way of doing things that allows us to work more effectively with families and schools. Perhaps some would refer to these as soft skills. Nevertheless, they are important. Developing an understanding of our school cultures, listening more than we speak, taking the time to understand and validate the perspectives of others, and knowing when to offer ideas that respectfully challenge families' and teachers' ways of thinking while helping them to support their children and students are invaluable characteristics of professionals who are committed to the well-being and success of young people.

REFLECTION AND DISCUSSION

1. At the end of Chapter 1, you considered your decision to become a teacher, administrator, school psychologist, school social worker, speech pathologist, or school counselor. Now, think about how you want others to view you in this role. How do you want to be perceived by parents, teachers, administrators, non-licensed staff, and students? Record your thoughts in the space provided below. If you are comfortable, share them with your classmates or colleagues.

2. How do the perceptions of students, families, and colleagues affect the degree to which we can effectively utilize our skills to fulfill our job responsibilities?

3. Identify at least one way in which you can serve students, families, or teachers while also learning more about your school culture and its surrounding community. Record your thoughts in the space provided below. If you are comfortable, share them with your classmates or colleagues.

4. A friend of mine who is also a principal told me this several years ago: *Charles, if there's one thing parents understand the first time you say it, it's what their children cannot do.* Reflect on the importance of this statement in your respective role as an educator. Being mindful of this reality, how can you be more sensitive to parents?

REFERENCES AND RESOURCES FOR PROFESSIONAL LEARNING

1. @JohnCMaxwell. (2018, Feb. 2). People don't care how much you know until they know how much you care. [Twitter post]. Retrieved from https://twitter.com/johncmaxwell/status/959458425599119365?lang=en

2. Erchul, W., & Young, H. (2014). Best practices in school consultation. In P. Harrison, A. Thomas (Eds.), *Best practices in school psychology: Data-based and collaborative decision making* (pp. 449-460). Bethesda, MD: National Association of School Psychologists.

3. Rogers, K., Schlitz, D., & Harvey, A. (1978). *The gambler*. Liberty.

4. Winfrey, Oprah. (Producer). (2004). *The Oprah Winfrey Show* [Television Series]. Chicago, Illinois: Harpo Studios.

5. Maslow, A. H. (1943). A theory of human motivation. *Psychological Review, 50,* 370.

6. @NicolasFerroni. (2014, Feb. 15). Students who are loved at home come to school to learn. Students who aren't come to school to be loved. [Twitter post]. Retrieved from https://twitter.com/nicholasferroni/status/434883769678327809.

CHAPTER 3

KEEPING THE MAIN THING THE MAIN THING:
SCHOOL PSYCHOLOGY, RTI, AND ASKING THE RIGHT QUESTIONS

> When a significant number of students are not making
> sufficient progress in the general education curriculum, the
> main thing is not our ability to design clever interventions
> and monitor progress. The main thing is redirecting our
> energy and resources to understand why this is happening.

Change is inevitable. For educators, it is continuously learning, as well as sharpening and refining our skills so that we are better prepared to serve students. The success of our respective fields hinges on remaining on the cutting edge of evidenced-based approaches. However, as we grow as individuals, and our disciplines become better equipped to meet the needs of all children, we must never lose sight of our fundamental purpose. To borrow a phrase from Stephen Covey (d. 2012), noted businessman and best-selling author of *The Seven Habits of Highly Effective People*[1], teachers, administrators, and school psychologists must keep the main thing the main thing.

THE QUESTION

In graduate school, I learned a principle that has significantly influenced my professional practice. Like a refrain that echoed throughout a medley of courses, my peers and I were often asked *what is the research question?* As school psychologists in training, we quickly realized that this simple query was central to all of our endeavors. In research, not only does the question inform the relevant literature that needs to be reviewed, critiqued, and synthesized, it also determines the participants, how they should be recruited, and the statistical procedures that are necessary to analyze a study's data.

Practitioners across disciplines regularly engage in activities that are driven by asking and answering specific questions. When students are performing below grade level expectations in reading, teachers want to know if their weaknesses are related to basic reading skills (e.g., letter-sound correspondence, phonemic awareness), sight word acquisition, fluency, and/or comprehension. Similarly, before observing students in classrooms and brainstorming interventions to promote their success, school psychologists must know the general concerns of families and teachers. Even when evaluating young people for a variety of educational disabilities, a clearly articulated question (i.e., the reason for referral) allows the design of assessment batteries that comprehensively and efficiently examine children's cognitive, academic, social, emotional, behavioral, and adaptive functioning.

THE APPROACH

Because change is inevitable, school psychology has matured since its inception. Despite our philosophical stance on identifying students with a Specific Learning Disability (SLD), this remains one of our primary responsibilities. Whereas the ability-achievement discrepancy model was once the prevailing practice, over time, Response to Intervention (RtI) has grown in its popularity and acceptance throughout the field.

Although there is empirical support for this approach, there are also limitations and challenges associated with implementing an RtI framework in schools. Beyond the realities of systems change and the availability of human capital to consistently provide evidence-based interventions to sometimes a significant number of students, many educators, including school psychologists, seem to neglect a fundamental premise of RtI. Through informally polling graduate students and colleagues about its critical features, many describe RtI as a tiered system of support that includes data-based decision making. While these responses are true, they are also incomplete in the absence of underscoring a foundational principle: quality Tier 1 (core) instruction. Admittedly, some argue that this goes without saying. Nevertheless, we should not assume that everyone understands this critical element upon which the model rests.

For quite some time, I have been thinking about data. As I often share with my undergraduate and graduate students, data is simply information that must be interpreted in context. Therefore, when presented with data about children's performance in school, what do we do with this information? In other words, are we asking the right questions? Specifically related to RtI, we are likely familiar with the three-tiered triangle that suggests 80 percent of students should meet grade level expectations through their exposure to core instruction (Tier 1); 15 percent require specialized intervention (Tier 2); and 5 percent could include students with disabilities who require the most intensive and individualized support in order to access the general education curriculum (Tier 3). While this premise is likely true, what about schools and school systems whose triangles may be inverted?

THE MAIN THING

Through its focus on systematic problem solving, school psychology aligns nicely with answering questions. However, the answers are only as helpful as our ability to ask the right questions. For schools that have large numbers of students who are not meeting grade level objectives, first, why is this happening? Next, what should we do about it? Although both questions are necessary, they are fundamentally different. To answer the second question, we may recommend providing students with Tier 2 interventions. Alternatively, to answer the first question we must critically examine the factors that explain why so many students are not meeting benchmark expectations.

In serving schools with significant numbers of English Learners (ELs) who are also from lower socioeconomic backgrounds, I have evaluated many of these students throughout my career. Generally referred due to not meeting academic expectations in the classroom or not passing end-of-year state assessments, I have noticed that their cognitive abilities are often commensurate with their same age peers and fall within the Average range. However, their academic skills (e.g., basic reading and reading comprehension, spelling and written expression, math computation and math problem solving) fall significantly below normative limits. These data have led me to ask the following question: *If students have generally Average cognitive functioning, why aren't they performing better academically?* Although I am not necessarily expecting all academic areas to fall within normative limits, the students that I am referring to had skills that were significantly below expectations (i.e., within the Borderline Deficient or Deficient ranges) in virtually all areas. If we believe that assessments of cognitive abilities are valid predictors of academic performance, it stands to reason that other factors are negatively affecting these students' skill development. Yes, second language acquisition, English language proficiency, as well as the other exclusionary factors for SLD are important to consider; but what happens when these have been adequately ruled out? When students, especially those who are culturally and/or linguistically diverse (CLD), are not making adequate progress in the general education curriculum, our first, or even second, thought should not be the suspicion of an educational disability.

Given the focus on RtI in recent years, albeit well-intentioned and grounded in solid science, it is worth considering the degree to which our efforts to support students are misguided by prematurely intervening without first addressing systemic factors such as the quality of Tier 1 instructional programming. In other words, are we asking the right questions? Rather than starting with what questions (e.g., what interventions can we provide to support students' decoding skills?), why questions may be more salient (e.g., why are so many students not meeting benchmark expectations?). Whereas what questions presume that the core instruction is of high quality, rigorous, effectively differentiated, and appropriately paced, why questions explore complex factors that are beyond students' control, but nonetheless contributory to their success in school.

In sum, I am not suggesting that RtI is ineffective to remediate students' academic skill weaknesses. In fact, some students require targeted interventions. I am, however, encouraging teachers, administrators, and school psychologists to carefully consider the following questions:

1. How do we know that our schools have high quality core instructional programs?
2. Especially for diverse learners, do our instructional programs include sufficient opportunities for differentiation in order to meet their cultural and linguistic needs?
3. If we have high quality core instructional programs, how do we know that teachers are implementing these programs with fidelity?

When a significant number of students are not making sufficient progress in the general education curriculum, the main thing is not our ability to design clever interventions and monitor progress. The main thing is redirecting our energy and resources to understand why this is happening. The main thing is addressing systemic barriers to ensure that all students have access to the highest quality educational experiences. In fact, more than universally screening and placing students in different tiers, which we do quite well, increased attention should be given to ensuring that all teachers are equipped to meet the needs of students who have diverse backgrounds and lived experiences.

CHAPTER SUMMARY

For school psychologists who are invested in improving outcomes for children, seeking to understand why before suggesting what is more than a semantic difference. It is fundamentally necessary in order to keep the main thing the main thing. A sensitive topic that we must be careful and thoughtful about discussing with teachers and administrators, disproportionately referring and subsequently identifying ELs with educational disabilities could be the result of ineffective instructional programming. In other words, despite excellent teachers using creative strategies to meet the needs of their CLD students, are they required to use curricula and programs that lack empirical support? As teachers, administrators, and school psychologists, if we believe that all students can learn, but some are not, we must critically examine why this is happening and correct our professional practice.

Although viewed as experts in the assessment and identification of educational disabilities, school psychologists can also make meaningful contributions to general education instructional programming and policies. Skilled in using data to inform decisions, school psychologists are prepared to assist schools and school systems in examining the evidence base of instructional programs used with all students.

REFLECTION AND DISCUSSION

1. With your school-based teams, discuss the extent to which your general education curricula are meeting the needs of all students. Are specific groups of students (e.g., EL/CLD, students with disabilities) less successful with these instructional programs than others?

2. Based on #1, how can instructional programming be improved for students who are not making adequate progress?

3. If your school has implemented an RtI model, what percentage of students are identified as Tier 1, Tier 2, and Tier 3? If these numbers are significantly different from the recommendations offered in the literature (i.e., 80, 15, 5), discuss possible reasons for these differences. Note: Try to avoid student- or family-centered variables such as cultural or linguistic difference and socioeconomic status (SES) as your primary explanations. While these factors are relevant, focus on your knowledge of effective instructional programming and teaching practices and how improvements in these areas can lead to better outcomes for students.

4. As a teacher, school psychologist, or graduate student, how can you increase your knowledge of effective general education instructional programming and teaching practices for various students? Because we can learn a lot from teachers, develop a plan (e.g., interviewing or observing a general education, special education, or EL teacher, spending time in different schools and classrooms) and share it with a colleague, classmate, administrator, professor, or practicum/internship supervisor for feedback and accountability.

REFERENCES AND RESOURCES FOR PROFESSIONAL LEARNING

1. Covey, S. R. (1990). *Seven Habits of Highly Effective People: Powerful Lessons in Personal Change.* New York, NY: Simon & Schuster.

CHAPTER 4

6 CONSIDERATIONS FOR UNDERSTANDING THE INSTRUCTIONAL NEEDS OF ENGLISH LEARNERS

A willingness to utilize a multi-modal and multi-informant assessment process that values the unique contribution of both quantitative and qualitive data to learn as much as possible about students and their families helps to prevent misunderstanding and misidentifying ELs as a function of cultural and linguistic difference.

According to a 2014 *Washington Post* article, ethnic and racial minorities were projected to be, for the first time in the nation's history, the majority of students attending public schools[1]. Referring to data released by the United States Department of Education, by 2022, minority groups will constitute 54.7 percent of the nation's public school students. For various reasons, including the location of graduate programs and the competency and experience of faculty, it is not uncommon for graduate students to complete their training without significant instruction in, or exposure to, effectively serving diverse children. Nevertheless, because demographic trends indicate that all educators will likely encounter students and families who represent cultural and linguistic backgrounds that are different from their own, all school psychologists, educational diagnosticians, speech pathologists, teachers, and administrators must grow in their ability to accurately differentiate between whether culturally and linguistically diverse (CLD) students' academic difficulty is functionally related to an educational disability, language difference, or a combination of these and other relevant factors.

While not meant to replace in-depth training and ongoing professional learning related to serving CLD children, the six points presented in this chapter are based on extensive experiences in public schools with significant numbers of English Learners (ELs) who are also from lower socioeconomic backgrounds. From a preventative perspective, the chapter provides foundational knowledge for educators serving ELs related to the process of second language acquisition and important considerations for multidisciplinary teams before referring CLD students for comprehensive evaluations due to the suspicion of an educational disability (i.e., Specific Learning Disability; SLD). Interested readers are encouraged to consult the *References and Resources for Professional Learning* at the end of this chapter to further develop their understanding of second language acquisition and assessing CLD students.

EL STUDENTS ARE FACED WITH THE CHALLENGING TASK OF SIMULTANEOUSLY LEARNING ENGLISH AND ACADEMIC INFORMATION

For native English speakers, it is relatively convenient to overlook the complexity of learning a language that seems to be governed by arbitrary rules and irregularity. For example, although words like *horse* and *worse* and *lord* and *word* look like they should sound the same, they do not. What about *head* and *heat* and *tear* and *tear* (e.g., *There is a tear in my eye* vs. *The cloth will tear*)? Or, *heart*, *beard*, and *heard* as well as *how* and *low*? There are many other examples of words that native English speakers seem to intuitively pronounce correctly.

But what about students whose primary languages are not English and are also much more predictable by following consistent vowel patterns and rules for singular, plural, masculine, and feminine words?

From a linguistic perspective, homonyms (two or more words that have the same spelling but different meanings such as *read* and *read*), heteronyms (words that are written the same but have different pronunciations and meanings such as *bow* and *bow*), and homographs (two or more words that are spelled the same but are not necessarily pronounced the same, and also have different meanings, such as *bass* and *bass*) likely make English rather challenging for second language learners, especially as they are simultaneously trying to acquire academic skills (i.e., reading, writing, and math) and content knowledge (e.g., science and history). Given the many rules, and even more exceptions to consider, ELs often depend on context clues to interpret sentences. However, because context clues are also culturally loaded (e.g., the student must possess the requisite background knowledge to understand specific references), their difficulty pronouncing words and interpreting sentences is not only demoralizing and frustrating, but they also remain at a disadvantage for understanding information and ultimately learning.

THE PROCESS OF SECOND LANGUAGE ACQUISITION

PRE-PRODUCTION

For all children learning their native languages, understanding what is said to them (receptive vocabulary) typically develops before they are able to commu-

nicate using words (expressive vocabulary). Similarly, during the pre-production stage of second language acquisition, ELs are developing their receptive
understanding of unfamiliar words. Notably, as they are not yet able to speak
the new language, this may also be referred to as the *silent period*. Especially for
teachers who are working with ELs in their classrooms, knowledge of this stage
of second language acquisition helps them to reframe their impressions, form
more appropriate expectations, and also provide the most relevant curricular
interventions and accommodations to foster academic success.

EARLY PRODUCTION

During the early production stage, children are able to speak in short phrases
(e.g., one or two words). While students in this period of language development may answer questions with yes or no responses, they are likely unable
to elaborate with additional details or specificity. For teachers working with
young people at this stage of second language acquisition, phrasing questions
in a yes/no or multiple-choice format is critically important for them to convey
their knowledge in a developmentally appropriate manner.

SPEECH EMERGENCE

During the speech emergence stage, children are able to communicate using
simple questions and phrases. Relatedly, known in the literature as **Basic
Interpersonal Communicative Skills (BICS)**, ELs in this stage of second language acquisition converse informally with peers and adults in English. For
example, educators working with second language learners who have adequate-

ly developed BICS likely observe and overhear them speaking to their peers in social settings (e.g., during lunch and recess) about non-academic topics. Research suggests that students naturally develop BICS between five and seven years[2] by being exposed to their English-speaking peers or watching television programs (e.g., cartoons) in English. However, one of the most common misconceptions about BICS is that educators mistakenly correlate these conversational language skills with academic success. In other words, because students are able to use English to talk about their favorite foods and the games that they enjoy playing, teachers may feel that their academic difficulties are not related to second language acquisition but something else (e.g., an underlying educational disability).

INTERMEDIATE FLUENCY AND ADVANCED FLUENCY

During the intermediate and advanced fluency stages, ELs are considered to function in a manner that is comparable to native speakers. Whereas BICS refers to their ability to informally converse in English, **Cognitive Academic Language Proficiency (CALP)** involves having a firm grasp of the requisite vocabulary to meaningfully engage with, and benefit from, academic instruction in English[3]. As the current literature suggests that students require up to 10 years to develop adequate CALP in the language of instruction, not only is it a more advanced skill than BICS, it is also very different. In many ways, CALP integrates both vocabulary and concepts which, depending on their cultural and linguistic background, may be unfamiliar to ELs. While some vocabulary terms can be simplified or translated into students' native languages, other concepts may not have an appropriate native language equivalent. As students are simultaneously developing CALP and learning academic information, it is important that educators are aware of the degree to which their difficulty understanding content is an artifact of second language acquisition and not within-child (e.g., disabling) characteristics.

After reading the vignette below, consider the following questions:

1. How is knowledge of second language acquisition relevant to understanding the student and his family?

2. Can you identify the various stages of second language acquisition that were mentioned above?

John is a six-year-old kindergarten student. His parents are from El Salvador and have been living in the United States for five years. Although John was born in Maryland, his parents could not afford to provide structured learning experiences for him by attending daycare or preschool before enrolling in his local elementary school. John's parents speak Spanish at home, although they are beginning to learn English through classes at a local community center.

At the beginning of the school year, John's classroom teacher reported that he was often very quiet. He seemed hesitant to participate in classroom activities, especially during whole group instruction on the carpet. Academically, his silence made it difficult for his teacher to assess his knowledge and skill acquisition (e.g., letter identification, letter-sound correspondence, rhyming). Socially, when John's peers tried to include him in various activities and games, he seemed interested but would not respond verbally. However, while he was sitting or standing away from them, John was often looking in their direction and wanted to see what they were doing.

As the year progressed, John's participation in social and classroom activities increased. Initially, he used short, one-word utterances to respond to his peers, which were followed by longer phrases and sentences. By the middle of the year, although John was initiating play with others, he only occasionally raised his hand to ask and answer simple questions about reading, writing, and math.

Throughout elementary school, John grew more confident in his ability to speak English. By fourth grade, John's teachers described his conversational English as "impeccable" and similar to a native speaker. While he had many friends, some of which he had known since kindergarten, and frequently socialized with his peers between activities and during less structured settings (e.g., lunch, recess, physical education), John was less likely to participate during highly structured instructional times. Moreover, despite making consistent progress since kindergarten, John continued to perform below grade level expectations in all areas of the curriculum (e.g., reading, writing, math, science, social studies) and inconsistently passed end-of-year state assessments. During parent-teacher conferences, John's mother and father agreed that his English was consistently progressing; however, unlike their son, they had few opportunities to practice their English with other native speakers. While at home and in the community with family and friends, John and his parents almost always spoke Spanish. Relatedly, they were often unable to assist him with homework assignments. Based on the quality of John's conversational English, his teachers often questioned why he was not demonstrating more progress in the general education curriculum. Near the end of fourth grade, John's classroom teacher and EL teacher referred him to the school's multidisciplinary problem solving team. Specifically, they were concerned about his academic difficulty despite his excellent conversational English skills.

In fifth grade, the problem solving team met with John's parents to discuss his progress on two occasions. Coupled with receiving EL services to support oral language development (e.g., pre-teaching academic concepts and building his academic vocabulary) since kindergarten, additional interventions were implemented to assist him with basic reading skills.

In middle school, periodic meetings were held with John's teachers and parents. Towards the end of sixth grade, he began to demonstrate more academic progress. For the first time, John passed each of the end-of-year state assessments. In seventh grade, his grades consistently improved from generally Cs to Bs and some As. Due to his success and not requiring specific interventions that were significantly different from best practices in teaching, John was dismissed from the problem solving team.

Having served schools with students like John (e.g., students who were born in the United States but whose parents are relatively recent immigrants who speak Spanish; students for whom kindergarten is their first structured learning experience; students who are learning English in kindergarten), his presentation and the perceptions of his teachers are relatively common. First, John's reluctance to speak in kindergarten, followed by using very short phrases, showed that he was in the early stages of second language acquisition. Over time, as he began to regularly interact with his peers in informal settings, John showed that he was developing BICS. However, his academic difficulties in the classroom and performance on end-of-year state assessments highlighted that he needed additional time to develop CALP.

Depending on why John's teachers referred him to the problem-solving team, their decision was not necessarily wrong. As educators who were concerned about his performance, it is possible that they were seeking to collaborate with other professionals to gain additional perspective and intervention ideas to support him in the classroom. However, if they were considering a referral for a comprehensive evaluation because they suspected that he had an educational disability, given the available data, such thinking would likely be premature. Their comments about the quality of his conversational English suggests that they were expecting him to perform better academically.

In sum, John's teachers were focused on his BICS (i.e., conversational English skills) without fully appreciating the necessary time to develop adequate CALP (i.e., academic language skills) in order to be successful in an English-only curriculum. As evidenced in the vignette, with increased time in English-speaking schools, John's CALP continued to improve. Eventually, his grades and performance on end-of-year state assessments in middle school showed that his CALP had developed to a level that facilitated greater success in the curriculum.

CRITICALLY EXAMINE STUDENTS' RATE OF PROGRESS IN ADDITION TO BENCHMARK PERFORMANCE

Although important for ELs, this principle is applicable to all students. In the era of data-based decision making and accountability, educators, including school psychologists, can become overly concerned with students' benchmark performance while losing sight of students as individuals. Like me, you have likely attended meetings in which you seem to be drowning in a sea of data as scores are presented about students' skills in several academic domains. At times these data points, which often have different scoring and scaling systems, are both overwhelming and confusing. I can only imagine how intimidating it must feel for some families to hear test names, acronyms, letters, levels, and numbers more than their children's names.

As educators, not only should we be mindful of sharing information with families that is understandable and relevant, but it should also help them have a better understanding of the skills that their children have already acquired as well as what they are currently working to develop. In addition to always sharing positive qualities about students before areas that need improvement, the following framework may be helpful for educators relaying information to families:

1. What does the student do well?

2. What is the student's specific weakness? For example, are the student's reading challenges related to difficulties with letter-sound correspondence, phonemic awareness, sight word acquisition, fluency, or comprehension? In math, is the student's difficulty related to completing multi-step computation problems, or poor recall of facts with automaticity? In writing, does the student possess good ideas, but struggle to document them on paper? Or, are there fine motor weaknesses that make writing physically laborious? Understanding students' difficulties with as much specificity as possible is very helpful for intervention development and subsequent progress monitoring.

3. What evidence-based strategies have been implemented to support the student's specific skill weakness? Or, what are some ways that

school-based staff and families can support the student's deficit?

4. If accommodations or interventions have already been implemented, what do the data show about their effectiveness?

After framing students' strengths and weaknesses, it is important to focus more on their rate of progress than their proficiency level (e.g., benchmark or grade level performance). In virtually all instances, the nature of problem solving team meetings is that the students who are being discussed are performing below grade level expectations. For ELs who may also have interrupted formal education, such performance is not necessarily surprising. Repeatedly highlighting this is less helpful than carefully analyzing the extent to which they are making, or not making, progress with implemented interventions.

Moreover, because typically developing monolingual students generally demonstrate approximately one year's progress within one year, this should be a guide for ELs. Additional research is necessary to better understand the expected rate of progress for ELs in various academic skill areas due to the complex interplay of CALP, prior educational experiences, and the appropriateness of general education programming and EL instructional models. Nevertheless, focusing on ELs' rate of progress provides teams with preliminary information as to whether their skill acquisition is relatively commensurate with typically developing peers. If it is, despite continuing to perform below grade level expectations, ELs are showing that they are learning at a rate that is consistent with their non-disabled peers and thus, may not be showing signs of SLD. Alternatively, problem solving teams should be more concerned when ELs are not only performing below grade level expectations, but their rate of progress is also slower than typically developing peers (e.g., making three-month's worth of progress within one year).

As Response to Intervention (RtI) becomes increasingly popular with schools and school systems, numerous progress monitoring tools are available to track student growth. Based on a variety of factors, including student age and the skill that is being targeted for intervention, schools can select an appropriate suite of tools for universal screening (i.e., baseline assessment) and progress monitoring. Many commercially available programs (e.g., Dynamic Indicators of Basic Early Literacy Skills (DIBELS)[4]; AimsWeb[5]; FastBridge Learning[6]) also include web-based scoring and a variety of data output formats to assist teams with interpretation and decision-making.

SOME EL STUDENTS' WRITTEN EXPRESSION ABILITIES WILL LIKELY BE THE LAST TO DEVELOP—THEY ARE AN INTEGRATION OF READING AND SPELLING SKILLS

As educators, we must resist the temptation to view ELs as monolithic. In other words, CLD students exist along a broad spectrum of diversity. For example, there are at least 12 types of ELs who are qualitatively different from their EL peers based on some of the following characteristics: place of birth; length of time in the United States; quality and consistency of prior educational experiences; and social and political conditions in their native countries that precipitated coming to the United States[7].

Relatedly, it is important for educators to appreciate the diversity of ELs' native language backgrounds. To measure and monitor their English language proficiency in the areas of Listening, Speaking, Reading, and Writing, and to help determine their eligibility for EL support services, some states use the *World-class Instructional Design and Assessment (WIDA) Assessing Comprehension and Communication in English State-to-State (ACCESS) for English Language Learners (ELLs) assessment*[8]. Depending on ELs' native language background, it is possible that their Listening and Speaking skills will develop faster than their Reading and Writing skills. Relatedly, some ELs will acquire basic skills (e.g., letter recognition and math computation) before more applied skills (e.g., reading comprehension and math problem solving) as the former is less dependent on linguistic factors. Importantly, however, this skill development sequence is not necessarily applicable to logographic languages (e.g., Chinese) in which glyphs or symbols represent words or morphemes. For students with these linguistic backgrounds, it is not uncommon for their written language skills to develop before their reading skills.

IN ADDITION TO WHAT IS PRESENTLY OBSERVED IN UNITED STATES SCHOOLS, GATHER INFORMATION ABOUT STUDENTS' ACADEMIC PERFORMANCE IN THE COUNTRY OF ORIGIN

It is extremely valuable for educators to spend time speaking with ELs' families about their previous educational experiences. Especially because some students arrive to our schools with incomplete academic records, if any, informal conversations between families and educators provide rich qualitative and contextual information about the similarities and differences between young people's performance in their native language/country of origin and English/United States schools. The questions presented below are suggestions for educators to ask families using a semi-structured interview format to better understand their students and inform instructional decisions.

1. Before moving to the United States, did your child attend school? If yes, how many days per week? How many hours per day?

2. At what age did your child begin attending school?

3. In what language(s) was your child's education provided?

4. Before arriving in the United States, have there been any interruptions in your child's education (e.g., not attending school for several weeks, months, or years)?

5. Before arriving in the United States, what type of school (e.g., public, private) did your child attend?

6. Before arriving in the United States, what were your child's grades while attending school? If you don't know your child's grades, please describe if your child experienced difficulty in the areas of reading, writing, or math.

LANGUAGE DIFFERENCE IS NOT SYNONYMOUS WITH DISABILITY

One of the most important responsibilities of school psychologists, educational diagnosticians, speech pathologists, teachers, and administrators serving ELs is contributing to discussions that help to accurately differentiate between whether students' academic difficulties are primarily due to language difference (e.g., second language acquisition), educational disability, or both. Having served CLD students throughout my career, arriving at the most appropriate decision is a nuanced process. While comprehensive evaluations of students' cognitive abilities and academic skills can be informative, before they are referred for these assessments, problem solving teams are encouraged to review data from a variety of sources to begin thinking about the degree to which second language acquisition is contributing to the difficulties observed in the classroom.

For ELs to be identified with SLD and eligible to receive special education support services, exclusionary factors—limited English proficiency, lack of appropriate instruction in reading and math, and environmental, cultural, or economic disadvantage—must be adequately ruled out as the primary determinants affecting their ability to access and make progress in the general education curriculum. While not explicitly referenced in federal regulations, culturally responsive clinical practice suggests that there should be evidence of disabling characteristics in the native language as well as English. In the absence of such data, educators should consider the extent to which students' performance is better explained as a function of language difference. A willingness to utilize a multi-modal and multi-informant assessment process that values the unique contribution of both quantitative and qualitive data to learn as much as possible about students and their families helps to prevent misunderstanding and misidentifying ELs as a function of cultural and linguistic difference.

CHAPTER SUMMARY

While the disproportionate identification of diverse students with disabilities has been frequently discussed by practitioners and researchers alike, the converse is also concerning. When diverse students with legitimate disabilities are not identified, they are being denied support services to which they are entitled in order to access the general education curriculum. As educators, we must ensure that ELs are not inappropriately identified or overlooked due to cultural and linguistic factors.

The increased diversification of the United States necessitates that serving ELs is not only for certain teachers (e.g., EL teachers), disciplines (e.g., EL departments), or those whose current school communities have significant numbers of CLD students. Fundamentally, public education is for all students. Therefore, all educators must be prepared to meet the instructional needs of diverse learners. Being a lifelong learner is not only applicable to students, but also educators who seek to do what is most appropriate for all children.

REFLECTION AND DISCUSSION

1. Of the six considerations presented throughout this chapter, choose one area in which you can increase your knowledge. Next, identify three actions that you can take to develop your knowledge of the instructional needs of English Learners. Record your thoughts in the space provided below. If you are comfortable, share them with your classmates or colleagues.

2. In thinking about the process of second language acquisition, brainstorm instructional strategies that might be helpful for students in their respective stages.

Pre-Production

Early Production

Speech Emergence

Intermediate Fluency

Advanced Fluency

3. What are some of the dangers of misunderstanding ELs' academic and behavioral presentation in school as being functionally related to an educational disability rather than language difference? Record your thoughts in the space provided below.

REFERENCES AND RESOURCES FOR PROFESSIONAL LEARNING

1. Strauss, V. (2014, August 21). For the first time, minority students expected to be majority in U.S. public schools this fall. *The Washington Post*. Retrieved from https://www.washingtonpost.com/news/answer-sheet/wp/2014/08/21/for-first-time-minority-students-expected-to-be-majority-in-u-s-public-schools-this-fall/?utm_term=.96454e52b4a8

2. Collier, V. (1987). Age and rate acquisition of second language for academic purposes. *TESOL Quarterly, 21*, 617-641.

3. Collier, V. (1989). How long? A synthesis of research on academic achievement in second language. *TESOL Quarterly, 23*, 509-531.

4. Cummins, J. (1984). *Bilingualism and special education: Issues in assessment and pedagogy.* San Diego: College-Hill.

5. Dynamic Indicators of Basic Early Literacy Skills. www.dibels.uoregon.edu

6. AimsWeb. www.aimsweb.pearson.com

7. FastBridge Learning. www.fastbridge.org

8. Wright, Wayne E. (2015). *Foundations for Teaching English Language Learners.* 2nd edition. Philadelphia, PA: Caslon, Inc.

9. WIDA. www.wida.us

To learn more about assessing culturally and linguistically diverse students, please consult the resources listed below.

1. Klinger, J. & Eppolito, A. M. (2014). *English language learners: Differentiating between language acquisition and learning disabilities.* Arlington, VA: Council Exceptional Children.

2. Lau, M. Y., & Blatchley, L. A. (2009). A comprehensive, multidimensional approach to assessment of culturally and linguistically diverse students. In J. M. Jones (Eds.), *The psychology of multiculturalism in the schools: A primer for practice, training, and research* (pp. 139-171). Bethesda, MD: National Association of School Psychologists.

3. Ortiz, S. O. (2014). Best practices in nondiscriminatory assessment. In P. Harrison & A. Thomas (Eds.), *Best practices in school psychology, VI: Foundations* (pp. 61-74). Bethesda, MD: National Association of School Psychologists.

4. Paradis, J., Genesee, F., & Crago, M. B. (2010). *Dual language development & disorders: A handbook on bilingualism & second language learning.* 2nd ed. Baltimore, MD: Paul H Brookes Pub Co.

5. Rhodes, R. L., Ochoa. S. H., & Ortiz, S. O. (2005). *Assessing culturally and linguistically diverse students: A practical guide.* New York, NY: The Guilford Press.

CHAPTER 5

SOCIAL JUSTICE:
A FRAMEWORK FOR EQUITY IN PUBLIC EDUCATION

> And whenever there is inequity, there is always a justice
> implication. When we adequately address the systemic
> injustice, in turn, we will effectively decrease inequities.

Like other industries, education is susceptible to trends and fads. Several years ago, diversity and diversity initiatives were buzzwords throughout education in an effort to increase the number of individuals from historically underrepresented backgrounds in our respective disciplines. But while diverse representation is important and necessary to serve students, it is not sufficient. Whereas diversity affords teachers, administrators, school counselors, school social workers, educational diagnosticians, speech pathologists, and school psychologists encompassing the spectrum of race, ethnicity, socioeconomic status (SES), gender, gender identity, age, language proficiency, disability, sexual orientation, and religious affiliation a seat at the proverbial table, having a seat does not mean that everyone enjoys their experience.

Over time, discussions that were once dominated by diversity have shifted to also include critical dialogue about equity. Eshé Collins, education attorney and member of the Atlanta Board of Education, states that "There is a major, but often overlooked, difference between equality and equity. For example, equality is making sure that every child receives the same pair of shoes. Equity, however, ensures that not only [does] every child receive the same pair of shoes, but they receive the size that fits them[1]." In other words, equity not only guarantees that diverse individuals are invited to sit at the table, but they also enjoy the same quality meal. Whereas diversity says, "Come over for dinner. I've saved a seat for you," equity says, "Don't worry about eating before leaving your house. There will be more than enough appetizers, salad, bread, entrees, and assorted beverages for everyone. In fact, upon arrival for dinner, you'll see that everyone's seat has been carefully arranged so that they can enjoy the evening's entertainment with an unobstructed view of the stage." This analogy highlights the principal distinction between diversity and equity: diversity wants everyone to be present. Equity, however, wants everyone represented to also have the same quality experience.

As research builds on previous studies, equity stands on the shoulders of diversity. Relatively new to some fields of education, social justice is the most recent iteration to the ever-evolving discourse about diversity, inclusion, and equity. While there are several definitions of this critically important construct, the *National Association of School Psychologists (NASP) Leadership Assembly* adopted the following conceptualization to frame the organization's commitment to social justice, not only as an ideal, but a central feature of the profession's research, practice, training, and advocacy: *Social justice is both a process and a goal that requires action. School psychologists work to ensure the protection of the educational rights, opportunities, and well-being of all children, especially those whose voices have been muted, identities obscured, or needs ignored. Social justice requires promoting non-discriminatory practices and the empowerment of families and communities. School psychologists enact social justice through culturally-responsive professional practice and advocacy to create schools, communities, and systems that ensure equity and fairness for all children[2].*

While many features of social justice are beyond the scope of this chapter, it is important to reinforce that it is not only a goal, but also a process. As a process, social justice requires a commitment to personal growth through deliberate introspection and professional learning. As a process, social justice is a way of thinking. It informs the manner in which we serve students and families who have been negatively affected by systemic injustice and oppressive power hierarchies. As a goal, social justice not only leads to equitable outcomes for everyone, but it is also everyone's responsibility.

SOCIAL JUSTICE FOR TEACHERS AND ADMINISTRATORS: DATA, DATA, DATA

One of the most challenging aspects of discussing social justice with educators is explaining it in a way that is practically useful and meaningful for their work with children. As someone who most closely identifies as a practitioner, I am particularly sensitive to my colleagues who may be somewhat skeptical of theoretical constructs that have been developed by researchers and seemingly lack relevance to their day-to-day service to students, families, schools, and communities. However, because social justice is informative for all educators, the information presented throughout this chapter seeks to demystify social justice.

Albeit subtle, schools and school systems are competitive. Even internationally, the United States is vested in its ranking in relation to other developed countries. From Connecticut to California and Mississippi to Maine, public institutions routinely report their high school graduation rates. Consider these data from one public school system for the Class of 2013: [School System] had an on-time graduation rate of 97.5 percent, which was 7.1 percent above the state average. Referring to the Class of 2014, the same jurisdiction boasted that 62.72 percent of its graduates would be attending a four-year college or university and 26.96 percent would be attending a two-year school. While these are impressive statistics that might allow the district bragging rights among its neighbors, these data can also overshadow students who are present in every public school system spanning the breadth of the United States. In light of what was reported, it remains that 2.5 percent of students did not graduate on time in 2013, and 8.34 percent of students would not be attending two- or four-year colleges or universities (1.98 percent planned to enroll in a branch of the armed services). Of the 4,540 graduates who comprised the Class of 2014, 378 young people would not be continuing their education.

Consider these data from the United States Department of Education, Office for Civil Rights[3]:

1. Black students represent 18 percent of preschool students, but account for 48 percent of students with more than one out-of-school suspension.

2. While Black students account for 16 percent of the public school population, 27 percent are referred to law enforcement agencies and

31 percent experience at least one school-related arrest.

3. Students with disabilities are more than twice as likely to receive an out-of-school suspension compared to their non-disabled peers.

Further, these data were released by the Annie E. Casey Foundation[4]:

1. Whereas 19 percent of children were living in poverty, Black and American Indian children were disproportionately represented at 34 percent, respectively.

2. While 65 percent of fourth graders were not proficient in reading, 81 percent of Black students, 79 percent of American Indian students, and 78 percent of Latino students were not meeting grade level expectations.

3. Similarly, whereas 67 percent of eighth graders were not proficient in math, 87 percent of Black students, 81 percent of American Indian students, and 80 percent of Latino students did not meet grade level objectives.

These examples underscore inequities in United States public schools that have been replicated in numerous peer-reviewed publications for decades. While some students are achieving, graduating on time, and continuing their education at institutions of higher learning, others are not. While some students disproportionately receive punitive disciplinary consequences, others do not. As alluded to throughout this book, disproportionality is an outcome. It is the result of systemic practices and policies that lead to young people experiencing public education in qualitatively different ways. However, because it is an outcome, disproportionality is also an opportunity to interrogate why some students remain in the margins of a high-quality education system while their peers excel. Social justice, which is more than theoretical rhetoric, provides a useful framework to engage in the necessary problem solving and subsequent actions to influence positive outcomes for children.

This chapter includes five recommendations to inform the clinical practice of school psychologists through the lens of social justice. Interested readers are encouraged to consult the *References and Resources for Professional Learning* at the end of this chapter to grow in their knowledge and understanding of social justice.

ASSESS CONTEXTUAL VARIABLES TO RULE OUT ALTERNATIVE EXPLANATIONS FOR CHILDREN'S PERFORMANCE

As practitioners, the principles of research design, specifically internal validity, are important. Consider the following example:

> Mrs. Ramirez teaches algebra at City High School. She is interested in whether a six-week afterschool tutoring program will improve her students' performance on the end-of-year exam in algebra. One day, Mrs. Ramirez allowed her class of 20 students to divide themselves into two equal groups. In addition to attending regularly scheduled algebra classes during the school day, Group A received 30 minutes of afterschool tutoring each week for six weeks. Group B did not receive extra math support but continued to attend regularly scheduled algebra classes during the school day. At the end of six weeks, all students were assessed using the end-of-

year exam in algebra. Somewhat surprisingly, the average score of students in Group B was significantly higher than the average score of those in Group A.

Based on the example above, one explanation for the informal study's results is that the afterschool tutoring intervention was ineffective for improving student performance on the end-of-year algebra exam. But while this is possible, there are several alternative explanations that are equally plausible to challenge this interpretation. First, because the students were allowed to choose their own group assignment, rather than being randomly placed into Group A or Group B, it is possible that the groups were unequal in students' math ability before the intervention began. In other words, the absence of random assignment could have led to more students who enjoyed math and/or excelled in math being in Group B compared to Group A. Next, because it is unknown if reasonable attempts were taken to ensure that the only difference between the students in Group A and Group B was their participation in the afterschool tutoring program, those in Group B could have used other supports (e.g., online remediation resources, parental assistance) to improve their math performance. Although there are additional limitations, the underlying premise remains: because there are alternative explanations that could account for the study's results, its internal validity—the degree to which the independent variable (i.e., afterschool tutoring) effects the dependent variable (i.e., performance on the end-of-year exam in algebra)—is questionable.

When school psychologists evaluate students for a variety of educational disabilities, they are seeking to uncover the reasons for their academic difficulty or functional impairment with a high degree of internal validity. In other words, does the disabling condition (e.g., Specific Learning Disability, Other Health Impairment, Emotional Disability, Autism)—and not other factors—account for why the student is not making progress in the general education curriculum? Consistent with Ecological Systems Theory[5], school psychologists who are committed to infusing a social justice lens into their professional practice understand that children are products of their interactions with multiple systems—microsystems, mesosystems, exosystems, and macrosystems. Appreciating the complex interplay among these systems, they seek to understand how stressors influence students as legitimate possibilities to counter premature within-child deficit models of disability. Before concluding that social, emotional, behavioral, and academic difficulties lie within the student, practitioners who are committed to social justice investigate, interrogate, and exhaust all relevant alternative explanations.

CHALLENGE THE STATUS QUO BY CONTINUALLY REFINING OUR PROFESSIONAL PRACTICE. WHEN NECESSARY, WE CHALLENGE THE PROFESSIONAL PRACTICE OF OUR COLLEAGUES.

Through presenting about assessing the cognitive abilities and academic skills of culturally and linguistically diverse (CLD) students to numerous audiences, I have learned that many practitioners are doing their best based on their training and experience. Personally, my professional growth in this area has been the result of critically examining the methods that I was using that unintentionally contributed to less equitable outcomes for students. In education, as in life, the problem with making mistakes is not the mistake in and of itself. Rather, it's refusing to grow beyond these missteps to do better after knowing better.

Together with my colleagues in Loudoun County Public Schools, we have developed a practitioner-friendly, empirically supported, multi-modal, and multi-informant co-evaluation model that has led to more accurately differentiating between language difference and educational disability[6]. Specifically, we engage parents and families to gather qualitative information about their children's language and educational experiences. We assess Cognitive Academic Language Proficiency (CALP), in both English and Spanish, to determine if students possess the requisite academic language skills to meaningfully participate in the general education curriculum. We think carefully about the academic achievement batteries that are used to assess CLD students' basic reading and reading comprehension, spelling and written expression, math computation and math problem solving, and listening comprehension and oral expression skills. Whenever possible, subtests with less cultural and linguistic demands are administered. Similarly, when assessing CLD students' cognitive abilities, we select instruments that have the smallest mean differences across racial and ethnic groups, lower cultural and linguistic loadings, and recommend a language reduced (e.g., nonverbal) estimate of students' functioning. Although these procedures have become systems wide policy for all school psychologists and educational diagnosticians, they are also regularly reviewed and modified based on effectiveness data.

RATHER THAN RELYING ON INCOMPLETE QUANTITATIVE DATA, GATHER QUALITATIVE INFORMATION FROM A VARIETY OF SOURCES

Practitioners who are committed to social justice recognize the limitations of relying on quantitative information to inform their impressions and subsequent decisions about students. After receiving behavior rating scale data about children's functioning across home and school settings, they view such information from parents and teachers as one element of a larger assessment system. Knowing that these instruments are subjective appraisals of children's functioning, practitioners who are committed to social justice corroborate quantitative data with other methods (e.g., comprehensive review of records, naturalistic observations in multiple settings, and interviews with parents, teachers, and children). Further, they understand that what is learned through face-to-face interactions often cannot be captured through behavior rating scales or standardized assessments.

For example, behavior rating scales are often included in the assessment of Attention Deficit Hyperactivity Disorder (ADHD) because they are acceptable to use, have been developed using large normative samples, are feasible for respondents to complete quickly, provide national comparison data for children of similar age and gender, and generally have strong psychometric properties[7]. However, it is important to consider the possibility that information provided through this methodology could reveal more about the raters themselves than the young people that are being evaluated. Because significantly elevated scores could have very different meanings for different raters (i.e., parents versus teachers), respondent interviews allow clinicians to understand their perspectives and ultimately arrive at the most appropriate diagnostic decisions. As the ultimate goal of assessment is not necessarily to uncover what is different about the child, a willingness to explore and examine other variables will inevitably lead to an equally important, albeit less considered question of assessment: why child behavior is perceived differently by different people.

REMAIN AWARE OF OUR PERSONAL BIASES SO THAT THEY DO NOT NEGATIVELY AFFECT STUDENTS

Following multiple acts of violence between non-majority individuals (i.e., Black men) and law enforcement, NASP released a statement condemning these atrocities coupled with ways that schools could model effective coping mechanisms and support its students[8]. Shortly thereafter, a diverse group of practitioners, faculty, and graduate students comprised the Social Justice Task Force (SJTF). For more than 18 months, the SJTF developed a variety of resources, including publications, infographics, lesson plans, and podcasts on topics such as privilege, implicit bias, and intersectionality to help school psychologists learn more about social justice and how to incorporate this framework into their practice while advocating for equity in their respective professional settings.

Having been intimately involved in these efforts with some of the leading social justice researchers and thought leaders in school psychology, the importance of individual responsibility, accountability, and introspection echoes throughout. While educators are committed to serving children, families, schools, and communities, we also have our own personal histories with racism, prejudice, discrimination, inequity, and systems of power and privilege that affect how we view the world. For this reason, we must allow ourselves the opportunity to wrestle with these constructs, first as individuals, before seeking to positively influence the lives of children. For suggested readings and activities on various topics that are related to social justice, please see the *References and Resources for Professional Learning* at the end of this chapter.

SEEK TO UNDERSTAND THOSE WHOM WE SERVE— THEIR RESPECTIVE HISTORIES AND CURRENT CULTURAL, SOCIAL, POLITICAL, AND ECONOMIC REALITIES

Coupled with serving an increasingly diverse student body are myriad issues facing children, families, and schools in their respective communities. As a result, practitioners who are committed to social justice make political statements on behalf of children.

As alluded to in Chapter 2, political is not necessarily synonymous with political affiliation (e.g., Democrat, Republican, Independent) or partisan politics. Instead, political statements are those that resist systems of power, privilege, and in many cases, oppression. Therefore, when educators and the professional associations to which we belong challenge systems, structures, policies, and practices that have negative effects on children, these are political actions. Whether comfortable or not, it is the nature of the world in which we live and what we are called to do as practitioners who are committed to social justice. Ignoring the larger social, cultural, and political contexts that affect children's lives is irresponsible. By broadening our perspective and adopting a whole-child paradigm, educators who are committed to social justice remain actively curious about young people and their histories to develop their knowledge and understanding of unfamiliar issues.

CHAPTER SUMMARY

Access to high quality public education is a fundamental right of all children. As highlighted throughout this chapter, a variety of factors lead to children having significantly different experiences in school. Such inequity is a matter of social justice. And whenever there is inequity, there is always a justice implication. When we adequately address the systemic injustice, in turn, we will effectively decrease inequities. Although tackling structural, societal, and systemic issues is necessary, it also takes time. However, as educators, we can commit to changing the manner in which we practice in order to improve outcomes for our students. By personally growing in our understanding of what social justice is, critiquing and challenging systems that lead to harmful practices and adverse outcomes for children, and incorporating a social justice lens into our service to students, families, schools, and communities, everyone has a part to play in advocating for the well-being of all children.

REFLECTION AND DISCUSSION

1. In your own words, explain the differences between diversity, inclusion, and equity. Record your thoughts in the space provided below. If you are comfortable, share these with your classmates or colleagues.

2. In your own words, define and explain social justice. Additionally, in your respective role as an educator, what does it mean to be committed to social justice? Record your thoughts in the space provided below. If you are comfortable, share these with your classmates or colleagues.

3. Review the *References and Resources for Professional Learning* at the end of this chapter. Identify one area in which you need to develop as an individual and as a professional. After reading at least one of the documents, record your thoughts and reactions in the space provided below. If you are comfortable, share these with your classmates or colleagues.

REFERENCES AND RESOURCES FOR PROFESSIONAL LEARNING

1. Atlanta Board of Education, Equity Retreat, November 11, 2014.

2. Adopted by the National Association of School Psychologists Leadership Assembly, September 2017. Retrieved from https://www.naspon-line.org/resources-and-publications/resources/diversity/social-justice

3. U.S Department of Education Office for Civil Rights (2014). *Civil rights data collection data snapshot: School discipline* (Issue Brief No. 1) Retrieved from https://ocrdata.ed.gov/downloads/crdc-school-discipline-snapshot.pdf

4. The Annie E. Casey Foundation. (2018). Report title. Baltimore, MD: Author. Retrieved from www.aecf.org

5. Bronfenbrenner, U. (1979). The Ecology of Human Development: Experiments by Nature and Design. Cambridge, MA: Harvard University Press.

6. Barrett, C. A., Cajas-Laynez, L., Parent, A., & Salguero, S. (2018). *For Us, By Us: Practitioner Guidance for Assessing Diverse Learners.* The Annual Convention of the National Association of School Psychologists. Chicago, Illinois.

7. Barkley, R. A. (2006). *Attention deficit hyperactivity disorder: A handbook for diagnosis and treatment.* 3rd edition. New York: Guilford Press.

8. National Association of School Psychologists. (2016). NASP statement regarding recent acts of violence. [Press release]. Retrieved from http:// www.nasponline.org/about-school-psychology/media-room/press-releases/nasp-statement-regarding-recent-acts-of-violence

To learn more about social justice and the work of the National Association of School Psychologists (NASP) in this area, please visit www.nasponline.org/ social-justice. Specifically, there are publications, infographics, lesson plans, and podcasts that help school psychologists and other educators grow in their understanding of privilege, implicit bias, intersectionality, and how these constructs affect the children, families, and communities we serve.

1. Implicit Bias: A Foundation for School Psychologists. National Association of School Psychologists. (2017). *Implicit Bias: A foundation for school psychologists* [handout]. Bethesda, MD: Author.

2. *Understanding Race and Privilege.* National Association of School Psychologists. (2016). Understanding Race and Privilege [handout]. Bethesda, MD: Author.

3. Understanding Race and Privilege: Lesson Plan and Activity Guide for Professionals. National Association of School Psychologists. (2017). Understanding Race and Privilege: Lesson Plan and Activity Guide for

Professionals [handout]. Bethesda, MD: Author.

4.   Talking About Race and Privilege: Lesson Plan for Middle and High School Students. National Association of School Psychologists. (2016). *Talking About Race and Privilege: Lesson Plan for Middle and High School Students* [handout]. Bethesda, MD: Author.

5.   Proctor, S., Williams, B., Scherr, T., Li, K. (2017) Intersectionality and School Psychology: Implications for practice. *Communiqué, 46,* 1, 19.

CHAPTER 6

IT'S ALWAYS ABOUT THE CHILDREN:
ADVOCACY, POLICY, AND SYSTEMS CHANGE

If it's not good enough for your children, it's not good
enough for other people's children.

From questioning whether I really wanted to become a school psychologist in
graduate school, to wondering how long I would remain in field and wrestling
with the dissonance between my emerging beliefs and some of the philosophical orientations that I encountered, I eventually found my niche in school
psychology. Because diversity and representation matter, I embraced the significance of my voice and unique perspective being a Black male in a field
that is predominantly White and female. Both personally and professionally
rewarding, I am grateful to have been afforded opportunities to influence the
manner in which school psychology is practiced to ultimately affect the lives
of children.

INVOLVEMENT IN PROFESSIONAL ASSOCIATIONS

Although I was not active in state and national associations as a graduate student, my participation as a practitioner has been eye-opening and life-changing. Not only are these organizations valuable for professional learning and networking opportunities, but they are intimately involved in developing and influencing policies that shape how school psychology is perceived and practiced at both the state and national levels. Importantly, these policies do not magically appear, but they are crafted with input from hardworking volunteer leaders—practitioners, faculty, administrators, and graduate students—who are relentless advocates and invested in the success of the profession by doing what is right for children. Because effective policies include the voices and perspectives of individuals representing the spectrum of diversity of our colleagues and the students, families, schools, and communities we serve, mentoring is essential.

MENTORING

Having a national perspective on school psychology has reinforced the importance of mentoring graduate students and early career professionals. Intentionally providing them with meaningful opportunities to serve not only ensures the continued vitality of the profession, but they are able to cultivate relationships that are pivotal for their future success.

The value of mentoring is captured in this simple phrase: seeing is believing. Graduate students see the possibilities of who they can become and what they can achieve when they are mentored by individuals, especially those who look like them or have similar backgrounds and life experiences. As it happened for me through Dr. DiGiuseppe, mentoring can change the trajectory of a student's life. While graduate school is instrumental for developing students as critical and independent thinkers, learning how to navigate the unspoken rules of the field and influence decisions is a matter of someone showing them the way. As a faculty member or experienced professional, if you aren't already, consider mentoring someone. As a graduate student or early career professional, if you are not being mentored, identify someone that you can learn from and continue growing into a well-rounded psychologist.

ADVOCACY, POLICY, AND SYSTEMS CHANGE

For most educators, including school psychologists, advocating on behalf of our students is natural. For example, teachers often ask building level administrators for time or other resources so that they can provide additional academic or behavioral interventions. And while we are often satisfied with ensuring the success of the students in our classrooms and schools, we can do more. However, many of us do not see ourselves as being able to influence systems and policies that affect all children.

Having attended the National Association of School Psychologists (NASP) and George Washington University (GW) Public Policy Institute (PPI), it was one of the most informative and helpful conferences of my career. More than receiving excellent information about special education law, education policy, and school psychology, I was equipped with practical strategies and empowered to begin influencing policy decisions at all levels of government—local, state, and federal. Note: The information that will be presented in the next section of this chapter was inspired by Kelly Vaillancourt Strobach, NASP Director of Policy and Advocacy, and Katherine Cowan, NASP Director of Communications, and serves as a guide to encourage educators to become advocates for all children[1].

KNOW WHAT YOU WANT

Advocacy begins with having a clear idea of what we want to accomplish. Yes, we are advocating for children; but what do we want specifically? What is our policy agenda? While the word agenda can be associated with negative connotations, it simply refers to what we want to achieve. For those of us who have worked with advocates in our respective schools, although challenging at times, advocates are fighting for what they believe is in the best interest of a child, which is what we should be doing as well.

After knowing what we want, we must do the necessary research to intelligently articulate and defend our positions. For whom is the issue or policy that we are advocating for important? Why is what we are fighting for important? Which individuals or groups may challenge what we want? As successful advocacy and policy advancement involve knowing who to influence, when educators understand the needs of various constituent groups (e.g., parents, central office administrators, school board members, and politicians) and frame their policy agendas to be responsive to as many audiences as possible, we will ultimately achieve greater outcomes for children.

Although we likely do not consider ourselves to be salespersons, we must become comfortable with convincing policymakers to support our advocacy goals. For school psychologists and others who use data to make decisions, we must know what works and translate research outcomes into implications that are relatable to everyday practice. For example, in advocating for additional school psychologists to support the social, emotional, and behavioral needs of students, highlighting how schools have become the de facto providers of mental health services through its access to large numbers of young people would be important. Showing how addressing these concerns leads to improved academic outcomes would also be helpful.

RECOGNIZE OPPORTUNITIES TO ACT

To influence systems, timing is everything. Effective advocates not only know what they want, but they also know when to ask for what they want. While we inherently believe that it is always the right time to do what is best for children, change is more accurately the result of the proper alignment of a problem with politics and policy. Always attuned to local and national events, successful advocates use these opportunities to underscore and advance their policy platforms. Using social media campaigns to build public consensus, persistently contacting legislative offices to garner political support, or sharing stories that foster authentic human connections between policymakers and children, successful advocates seize the moment to eloquently explain why change is necessary.

BUILD STRATEGIC RELATIONSHIPS

Fundamentally, change is a slow process that is dependent on relationships. Especially because the changes that we are fighting for are often at the systems level, there are no lone rangers in advocacy. To the greatest extent possible, educators partner with state and national associations within their respective disciplines and build strategic alliances with professionals in related organizations. As bridge and consensus builders, successful advocates bring stakeholders together representing diverse ideas and perspectives to not only capitalize on the strength of numbers and increased resources, but to also collaboratively work towards a common goal on behalf of children. Understanding how decisions are made, successful advocates are politically informed and savvy enough to know where power and influence lie to ultimately impact systems.

GATHER EVIDENCE

For those of us who are practitioners, we have a lot to offer the field. Despite the perception that research should inform practice and policy, good policies are also the result of effective clinical practice. While serving real children and families who attend real schools in real communities, it is important to collect data on the effectiveness of our programs and practices. Such information is tremendously valuable to inform policy implications for other practitioners.

USE CONSISTENT, EFFECTIVE COMMUNICATION

Central to effective messaging is knowing our audience and how to frame our advocacy efforts in ways that are meaningful to diverse stakeholders. Pragmatically speaking, we must make our policy agendas relevant to policymakers. Ensuring that they know what we are asking for, why it is important, as well as its benefit (e.g., the wow factor) further increases its appeal. Rather than simply glorifying the problem, successful advocates have a coherent answer that can be incorporated into a systems wide policy.

ENGAGE AND EVALUATE

Advocacy and policy are iterative processes. Like good science is constantly reviewed, critiqued, and refined based on data, after policies have been implemented they need to be evaluated for their effectiveness. As consumers of research, educators are invested in knowing if the policies for which they have advocated are achieving the desired outcomes for children.

CHAPTER SUMMARY

Policies provide frameworks that guide what we do as educators. Informed by evidence-based research and effective clinical practice, they are instrumental in promoting positive outcomes for students, families, schools, and communities. Because serving children includes speaking up for what is in their best interest, if we are not influencing systems that affect all children, we are not making progress as a profession.

Some of us may not know where to start in advocating for systems change. Which cause should we tackle? Which issues are most important to young people in our communities? While there is no single answer to these questions, consider the following statement: if it's not good enough for your children, it's not good enough for other people's children. In other words, advocacy is selfless as it ensures that all children have access to what we would want for our own families. The hope of today and the promise of tomorrow, everything we do—our instruction, our prevention and intervention efforts, our assessment practices, and systems wide policies—is always about the children.

REFLECTION AND DISCUSSION

1. If you don't have one already, identify at least three individuals that you would like to serve as your mentor. Record their names in the space provided below. If you don't have their contact information, ask your colleagues or professors—school psychology is a relatively small world. If you can't think of anyone that you would like to mentor you, ask your colleagues or professors for suggestions based on your professional goals (e.g., research, teaching, practice, administration). Be sure to follow-up with potential mentors.

2. Think about what is happening to the children in your school or community. Do all students have access to the necessary resources to receive a quality education? How are families being treated in your community? What are their living conditions? Identifying challenges and learning more about the factors that are contributing to these issues leads to advocacy opportunities. Next, follow these steps to begin your quest for change:

   1. Contact your discipline's (e.g., teachers, school psychologists, school counselors, school social workers) state and national associations to learn more about what they may already be doing to address the issue.

   2. Contact state and national leaders in your discipline's professional associations to learn more about how you can get involved with supporting advocacy efforts related to the issue.

   3. Recruit others—colleagues, graduate students, university faculty—to support your advocacy efforts.

3. Although the federal government has a role to play in public education, many decisions are made at the local (i.e., city, county, district) and state levels. If you don't already, how can you develop relationships with elected officials (e.g., school board members, senators, representatives) to ensure that they are aware of the issues that are facing children, families, schools, and communities? Record your thoughts in the space provided below. Be sure to follow-up with your elected officials.

REFERENCES AND RESOURCES FOR PROFESSIONAL LEARNING

1. Strobach, K. V. & Cowan, K. (2018). *Advocacy: The Role of Grassroots Advocacy in Policy Solutions.* The 2018 GW/NASP Public Policy Institute. Washington, DC.

2. Marian Wright Edelman is empowering the next generation of change-makers/ (2018, May). *HuffPost.* Retrieved from https://www.huffington-post.com/entry/marian-wright-edelman-is-empowering-the-next-generation-ofchangemakers_us_5a6f3432e4b06e253269d4cd

AFTERWORD

Children are resilient. They possess tremendous strength to adapt and adjust to difficult situations that they did not create. Whether being born into less than ideal circumstances or witnessing numerous tragedies in their schools and communities, their ability to rise above unfair odds is nothing short of remarkable. By organizing protests and demonstrations for fair treatment at the hands of law enforcement or demanding that their elected officials make common sense decisions so that their schools are safe and free from gun violence, young people have been responding to societal ills with courage, conviction, and intelligence.

Although children have been doing what adults have failed to do for them does not mean that we should place them in positions that force them to demonstrate such strength. Rather than expecting them to prematurely come to terms with weighty issues such as injustice and inequity, children deserve to enjoy the innocence of childhood that is found in being carefree and protected by the adults in their families, schools, and communities.

In some ways, the central message of this book can be captured in the following statement: doing what's best for children may be inconvenient for us. Because we are human, despite our desire to serve faithfully, at times we are discouraged. At times we are tired. At times we are frustrated and overwhelmed. But while these feelings are real, they pale in comparison to making meaningful connections to students, partnering with families and teachers in support of positive outcomes, continually growing as individuals and refining our professional practice, identifying and challenging injustice, and advocating for systems change on behalf of children.

As members of the most noble and honorable profession of all, if we aren't the voice for children, who will speak for them? If we aren't their champions, who will advocate for them? If we aren't the ones to challenge systemic injustice, who will protect them? Because it's always about the children, if we don't make everything we do about the children, who will?

The children are going to frame the future of this

nation. We need to empower [their] voices, and be

there with those voices, and build a world, a nation

that's fit for them[2].

—Marian Wright Edelman

Made in the USA
Middletown, DE
08 August 2022

70860367R00060